# LIMEKILNS

# AND LOBSTER POTS

*Two Beadnell fishermen: Stephen Douglas and his uncle William (Bill) Douglas, c 1969. Bill left school aged 13 in 1893 to join the family boat, and was still working at the age of 90. He was Fisheries Officer for the Northern Region for 32 years.*

*(Previous page) Beadnell Harbour c1900.*

# LIMEKILNS
# AND LOBSTER POTS

*A Walk Around Old Beadnell*

Katrina Porteous

ISBN 978-0-9565495-5-6

Published by Windmillsteads Books
an imprint of Jardine Press Ltd:
info@katrinaporteous.co.uk
www.jardinepress.co.uk

First published in 2013
Book design by Catherine Dodds
Printed by Potts Print (UK) Ltd, Cramlington, Northumberland

# CONTENTS

Two views of the Benty, taken about 60 years apart. The top photo, from between the Wars, shows small hay-cocks, or 'kyles', in the field, part of the farmyard, and cobles hauled up on the grass. It epitomises Beadnell's traditional occupations, farming and fishing. The lower photo, taken c1994, shows houses being built (left) on the site of Bent Hall farmyard.

# LIMEKILNS
# AND LOBSTER POTS

## *A Walk Around Old Beadnell*

*This is a circular walk of between two and three miles in length. A sketch-map showing the route may be found inside the front cover of this book. Landscape features and buildings are gathered into twelve areas of interest, numbered on the map. The text should help you locate features in the vicinity of each stopping-point. The map and descriptions are approximate; Beadnell is constantly evolving, and details might change after the date of publication.*

*Reference is made throughout to a plan of 1759 showing the estate of the landowner Thomas Wood, surveyed by James Robertson of Alnwick. Held among the Craster family papers in Northumberland Archives, Woodhorn (NRO ZCR 5), this makes a fascinating comparison with present-day Beadnell. It is reproduced by kind permission of the Craster family inside the back cover of this book.*

*Enjoy your walk but please, at all times, keep to marked footpaths and respect private land.*

# 1. START YOUR WALK
# FROM BEADNELL CAR-PARK

Behind you, in the distance, roughly half a mile to the north, you will see the spire of St Ebba's Church, surrounded by trees. This is the heart of the old village, or 'toon'. At the end of the 19th century, Beadnell was a village of just 67 households. The first edition Ordnance Survey, c1860, shows that one group of houses was concentrated around the church, with nothing between the 'toon' and the harbour except three small clusters of cottages scattered along the sea front. These were Beadnell Square, Windmill Steads and Bent Hall. Over the last century, the fields around these distinct clusters of cottages have filled in with houses, and Beadnell has grown into one continuous settlement. The wider parish now consists of around 450 households. More than half the houses in the village are second homes.

Why did Beadnell develop in this way? Our walk will follow a circular route, taking in the harbour and the 'toon', and visiting the sites between them, to try to answer that question, before returning across open fields to the car-park.

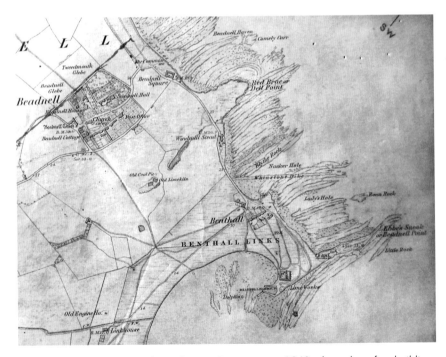

The first edition six inch scale Ordnance Survey map, c1860, shows how few buildings stood between Beadnell village and the harbour.

Beadnell c1900, from the old limestone quarry on the edge of the present Longstone estate. This picture shows, from left: the Town Farm stackyard before the new school was built; Meadow Lane ('the Lonnen'); Church Row; and St Ebba's House.

A view across the links to the Benty, c1930, showing only a few isolated houses on Harbour Road. In the foreground children play on the 'rocket post', used by the Volunteer Lifesaving Company to practise their drill (see pp54-5).

## Beadnell in the Anglo Saxon and Medieval Period

Beadnell, once known to its inhabitants as 'Beadlin', takes its name from the Anglo Saxon 'Bede's Hall'. The earliest written reference is found in 1161. Bede was a man's name, but the word could also refer to a 'beadsman' or man of prayer. The possible relevance of this will become clearer during our walk. In the Anglo Saxon period and throughout the centuries which followed, the settlement looked to Bamburgh as the centre of authority. Bamburgh was the royal capital of the powerful Anglo Saxon kingdom of Northumbria. After the Norman Conquest and throughout the medieval period, Beadnell was part of Bamburgh demesne. This meant that people who lived in Beadnell were tenants of the Lord at Bamburgh, and owed him many days of labour throughout the year.

During this period many of the inhabitants of Beadnell worked in the common fields. Others were fishermen. Fishing was a distinct profession by at least the 14th century. Herring, caught in summer, were dried, pickled or smoked; white fish, which was more valuable, were sold fresh, salted or dried. The Beadnell fishermen paid tithes (taxes) on fish to the monks at Bamburgh. 'Bednelfysch' (fish from Beadnell) also appears regularly in the accounts of Durham Priory and its dependency, Finchale Priory. Both bought Beadnell fish throughout the medieval period. Occasionally the Prior of Holy Island sent Beadnell fish to the monks of Durham as a gift. Although it is not clear what kind of fish these were, they were of high value; probably fresh cod or codling. In 1389, for example, Durham Priory bought 80 Beadnell fish each week for two weeks at 5s per week, then 60 Beadnell fish each week for the next four weeks at 3s 6d per week.

*Beadnell was a fishing village from medieval times. Its character changed in the 19th century with the industrialisation of the summer herring fishery. This picture shows herring keelboats in the harbour c1900.*

In 1538, around the time of the Dissolution of the Monasteries by Henry VIII, a royal survey listed 71 able-bodied men living in Beadnell. Nearly 100 years later, in 1626, Beadnell was said to have 14 resident fishermen, compared with only half as many at North Sunderland (Seahouses).

## Enclosure

At the beginning of the 18th century the Lord of the Manor of Bamburgh was Ferdinando Forster, a Jacobite sympathiser. His sister, Dorothy, was married to Bishop Crewe of Durham. The Forster family had many branches, several of which held land in Beadnell at different times. In 1701 Ferdinando and the other local landowners agreed to the enclosure of the common lands, including those at Beadnell. At the same time, Ferdinando confirmed the rights of fishing and bait gathering. Shortly after this he was murdered in Newcastle by John Fenwick of Rock. His bankrupt estate was bought up by his brother-in-law, Bishop Crewe. Lands belonging to other members of the Forster family, including the Beadnell Hall estate, and lands which had once belonged to the Harbottle family, were acquired in 1735 by the Wood family of Presson, a hamlet on the Tweed. This family features largely in the story of Beadnell's development.

*A Beadnell sailing coble in the Haven c1900. Sailing cobles of this kind were the traditional fishing boat of the Northumbrian coast. Unlike keelboats, they were regularly launched from the beach. They did not require a harbour.*

*Walk onto the beach from the car-park through the pedestrian entrance and, turning left, head to the harbour with its imposing limekilns.*

Like all Northumbrian fishing villages, Beadnell was known for its 'characters'. People worked very hard, often for little money, but shared a strong sense of purpose and community. The photo above shows (l-r) fishermen Tommy Liddell, Hugh Patterson (obscured), Jack 'Teedle' Dixon, Bob Fawcus and Charlie 'Steen' Stephens at the harbour c1928. The one on the left shows Mary Jane Liddell, Bella Fawcus and Bet Hall mending a salmon net at the Benty in the 1920s.

# 2. BEADNELL HARBOUR AND LIMEKILNS

Beadnell limekilns – now, like the harbour, a Grade II listed structure – were begun in 1798 at the instigation of the local landowner, John Wood. The harbour was built around the same time. Beadnell's rocky foreshore to the north of where you stand consists primarily of 'points' of Carboniferous limestone around 300 million years old, layered with sandstones, and containing coal measures. Together, coal and limestone can be burnt to produce lime, while sandstone is a useful building material. Thomas Wood, John's father, whose family bought land in Beadnell in 1735, saw an opportunity for the commercial exploitation of these rocks.

Thomas Wood leased out the rights to quarry stone and erect limekilns in Beadnell in the 1740s, but those early kilns were not here at the harbour. We shall see them later in the walk. The quarrying and lime-burning industry, and the coal mining needed to burn lime, had already been flourishing in the village for 40 years when John Wood took back the leases and sought an estimate for 'a new harbour at Ebb's Sneuk'.

*This photo of herring boats unloading their nets in Beadnell harbour, c1900, shows a serious crack in the southern limekiln. The kilns were used for lime-burning in the early 19th century, but seem to have largely ceased operation by the 1820s.*

Like his father, John Wood was an entrepreneur. England was in the throes of the industrial revolution at this time, and nearby Seahouses was developing its own quarrying and lime industries. North Sunderland (Seahouses) harbour was built c1788 for the export of lime, stone and grain. Estimates for a new harbour at Beadnell were obtained shortly afterwards, and work seems to have begun in the years which followed. In 1798 Wood leased the rights to coal and stone in Beadnell to Richard Pringle, and Pringle was given permission to construct a limekiln on the new pier, and to finish the harbour which, it seems, was intended primarily to serve the lime and stone industries. The first edition Ordnance Survey, c1860, shows a 'dolphin' a little way from the harbour mouth. This was a structure of stone and wood, which was used to moor ships or help manoeuvre them into the harbour with hawsers. The harbour was repaired and altered in the 19th century.

## Limekilns

Beadnell limekilns consist of a group of three kilns, built in more than one stage. It seems that the central kiln was built first, with a kiln added on either side afterwards. Part of the southernmost kiln has now fallen away. Limestone was brought to the top of the kiln by means of a horse-drawn tramway from quarries at Ebb's Sneuk and Bent Hall, along what is now Harbour Road. It was fed into the kiln with layers of coal from the local pits and burned at temperatures of around 1000 degrees centigrade. The resulting quicklime was shovelled out of the eyes at the bottom of each kiln and exported from the harbour in sailing boats called 'sloops'. Some lime was used for building, but most was used as an agricultural fertiliser. Much of the trade was with Scotland, especially with the port of Dunbar.

The lime industry was important to Beadnell's development, but it did not flourish for long. It began to decline at a time of rapid expansion of another industry with which Beadnell is more typically associated – fishing; and in particular, one branch of it: the herring industry.

*A rare photo showing the limekilns before restoration.*

8

The limekilns were given into the protection of the National Trust by Miss Amy Craster in 1935. This photo from 1950 was taken after restoration work to consolidate part of the southern kiln. It shows cobles, moored in the harbour now that it was no longer used by bigger boats. They include (l to r): Bob Hall's Quest, John Percy Douglas' Sweet Promise, Tom Fawcus' Sunbeam, Bill Dixon's Joan Dixon, Bob Douglas' Welcome Home and Robbie Douglas' Golden Gate.

The current profile of the limekilns from the south-east, with the interior of the southern kiln visible, and 'rock-armour' added by the National Trust for protection.

## The Northumberland Branch of the British Fisheries

John Wood was keen to organise Beadnell's fishing on a more commercial footing. Taking his lead from the British Fisheries Society, established in 1786 to build fishing stations in the Highlands and Islands of Scotland, Wood set up 'The Northumberland Branch of the British Fisheries' in 1788 with an ambitious group of investors. Trade centred upon Beadnell and Ullapool. The organisation bought boats and gear for the fishermen and disposed of their catch. The high-value catches of white fish and lobster were exported to London live in smacks, which moored in the natural havens between Beadnell's rocky points.

*This photo of Beadnell harbour from c1900 shows three of the village's ten keelboats: Tom Liddell's Harmony BK867, Bob Fawcus' Eunice BK1037, and 'Dode' Hall's Eon BK1055.*

## The Herring Industry in Beadnell

Herring is a migratory fish. Shoals travel south from Northern Scotland in spring to East Anglia in autumn. Herring had been caught in summer on the Northumberland coast for as long as men had fished; but it had always been regarded as a low-value catch, because it was abundant, and because, as an oily fish, it was quick to spoil. The old methods of preserving it included salting, and smoking for many days at a time. In the late 18th and early 19th century, however, improved methods of preserving herring were introduced on the Scottish East Coast. This opened up a massive market for herring in the Baltic. Scottish methods rapidly spread into Northumberland and John Wood was quick to invest

10

in them. For the next 100 years Northumberland's coastal villages – even small villages like Beadnell – supported a busy summer herring fishery which could properly be described as an industry.

Beadnell's herring fishing began in June and ended in September. The herring were caught at night, when they rose to feed. Rather than using small cobles, fishermen pursued herring using larger 'keelboats' of 40 to 50 feet in length, crewed by six men. These boats usually fished close to home, for one night at a time. They fished with 'drift nets', which were attached to the boat at one end and hung down like a curtain in the water. These were left to drift with the tide for several hours, then hauled by hand, or with a winch; either a hand-operated 'iron man' or a steam capstan. Once caught, to maintain quality, the herring had to be rushed ashore as quickly as possible for processing.

*Herring keelboats leaving Beadnell harbour in the early evening, c1900. In the picture of the single keelboat (above), two of the crew operate the capstan or 'iron man' to hoist the sail.*

*Some herring keelboats used a steam capstan to replace the hand-operated 'iron man'. The abandoned boiler from one such capstan is periodically visible in the sand beside Beadnell harbour.*

John Wood built a large herring house at his new harbour in Beadnell in 1800. Herring yards were run by 'coopers', who made the barrels and oversaw the work. Wood leased his new herring house to coopers from Berwick, and by 1821 he was allowing two Berwick men, Hill and Ormston, to use one of the three limekilns for herring curing. Six years later, he built a further set of herring yards. By this time, boats from the East Coast of Scotland, Ireland, Cornwall and the Isle of Man were arriving at Beadnell at the height of the herring season. There were times when the bay was thronged with boats. In 1828 Wood wrote to Trinity House about a storm which had resulted in 'near one thousand poor fishermen in open boats' taking shelter in the bay. At that time Trinity House regarded Beadnell as 'the central point' for the herring fishery, and allowed Wood to display a lantern on Ebb's Sneuk Point during the season.

John Wood died in 1828. Hill the fish curer died three years later. In the years following these deaths, a dispute over the lease of the kilns meant that they and the harbour fell into disuse, and by 1836 the harbour was described as 'ruined'. This was the reason why Seahouses so quickly overtook Beadnell as a centre of importance in the herring industry, and why that village continued to flourish and expand in comparison to Beadnell. Although Wood's son, Thomas Wood Craster, repaired Beadnell Harbour, and although it continued to be used for the herring industry, for stone and gravel shipments, and even, during a brief revival in the 1840s, for lime export, its upkeep presented problems. The harbour was costly to maintain and constantly filled with sand.

(Above) Dredging the harbour by hand, c1900. To this day, Beadnell harbour needs to be dredged annually to prevent it filling with sand.

(Right) In the heyday of herring fishing, some Beadnell fishermen followed the herring shoals to Great Yarmouth and beyond. Tom Hall, pictured here c1900, travelled to Ireland in his herring boat, the Hephzibah.

The herring industry continued in Beadnell until just before World War I. In the first decade of the 20th century, nine or ten Beadnell fishermen still owned herring keelboats of between 40 and 50 feet. These included Tom Baxter Douglas' *Iona*, Ralph Dixon's *Excellent*, John Douglas' *Lady Elcho*, Tom and John Douglas' *Ann*, Bob Fawcus' *Eunice*, John 'Aa'd Weir' Fawcus' *Britannia*, George 'Dode' Hall's *Reliance*, Tom Hall's *Hephzibah*, Robert Handyside's *Advance* and Tom Liddell's *Harmony*. Part of the 'yard', or spar, which carried the sail of the *Lady Elcho* now forms a mooring post on the south pier.

Beadnell's herring season was short, and by 1900 catches were falling. Fishermen blamed the new steam trawlers, which caught white fish, for destroying the herring spawning grounds on the sea bed. In addition, prices were low, sometimes as little as two shillings a barrel, which did not even cover the price of transportation to market. When there was a glut of herring they were impossible to sell. Fishermen were often obliged to dump their entire catch. At the same time, fishermen from Eyemouth and North Shields were investing in new steam drifters to catch herring; but Beadnell, with its tiny harbour, could not accommodate these bigger boats or afford the investment for so short a season. So a century of industrialised herring fishing had all but ended in Beadnell when World War I dealt it a final

*Keelboats abandoned on the beach in the early 1920s, some years after Beadnell's herring fishing ended. It is said that these two, Bob Fawcus' Eunice BK1037 and Dode Hall's Reliance BK21, still lie beneath the sand.*

blow, closing the Baltic markets. From that time onwards, Beadnell fishermen reverted to their small cobles and to the artisan forms of fishing which had for centuries sustained them – crabs, lobsters, turbot, salmon, and their staple, the long line fishery for cod and haddock. Beadnell's herring keelboats were turned into sheds, or left to rot on the beach.

## After World War II

Without regular dredging, Beadnell harbour rapidly filled up with sand. It remained the property of Wood's successors, the Craster family, until 1949, when Sir John Craster gave it to the Beadnell Harbour Fishermen's Society, to which it still belongs. Shortly afterwards, the harbour entrance was further narrowed. The extension incorporates some of the concrete blocks which were used on the beach to deter invasion during World War II. Close examination of the concrete reveals graffiti from that time.

*Beadnell harbour, seen here full of sand after World War II. The cobles include Tom Fawcus' Sunbeam BK224.*

## Harbour in Trouble

The harbour has always required continuous investment to maintain it. In 1997 its south wall collapsed, and towards the end of that year the damage worsened. The following year the Harbour in Trouble appeal fund was launched by village residents, whose hard work raised £30,000. Central and local government then stepped in with funding of £300,000, and repairs were completed in 2001.

The hole in the harbour's south wall, 1998, with the Douglas' coble the Golden Gate BK221 in the foreground.

## Beadnell Harbour Today

Today there are three boats fishing from the harbour, including one motor coble from Craster. These boats catch crabs and lobsters; they do not fish for white fish or herring. Sea-trout and salmon are also caught in summer. During the months of May to August it is often possible to watch fishermen catching sea-trout in the bay using beach nets anchored close to the shore. Locally caught shellfish, and salmon in season, may be bought fresh from Swallow Fish on South Street in Seahouses or from Robsons' in Craster. It is also served in local pubs and restaurants: ask for what is available. Beadnell is still a fishing village, and by enjoying its produce you help to retain its character and support the local fishermen.

*Fishing is a dangerous occupation, and the sea around Beadnell has seen many tragedies. This photo shows the funeral procession for fisherman Dick Hall, drowned with his son William at their salmon nets in Beadnell Bay on July 2nd 1921.*

## A West-Facing Harbour

Beadnell harbour is said to be the only one on the East Coast to face west. The bay curves away, backed by sand dunes, the largest of which has been known since at least the 17th century as 'Featherblaa'. The offshore rocks are known as 'the Carrs', and beyond them, where the dunes dip down, the Long Nanny burn runs into the sea. In the 18th century, popular horse races were run along these sands until, in 1794, one of the riders was killed. The races were moved to Belford in 1826.

Besides lime, stone and herring, another important export from Beadnell harbour was grain. John Wood was one of several Northumberland estate owners who invested heavily in agricultural improvement in the late 18th century. As a result of this increased enterprise, cereal cultivation flourished in the area, soon exceeding local demand. Arable farmers invested in transport and shipping, and ports such as Alnmouth prospered. The agricultural settlements of Swinhoe and Tughall, close to Beadnell, had ground their grain at Tughall Mill on the Long Nanny burn since medieval times. Folk memory recalls that grain exported from Beadnell harbour was led along the sands by horse and cart from Tughall Mill, through what was known as 'The Miller's Nick' in the dunes. Grain was also stored in newly-built granaries in Beadnell 'toon' and at Bent Hall.

*Before you leave the harbour, walk to the south-east corner of the outer pier, from where you can look out towards Dunstanburgh Castle.*

## The Old Pier

Robertson's map of Beadnell, published in 1759, before the present harbour was built, shows an 'old pier' extending south-west from the corner of the present harbour. At low water the L-shaped footings of this pier, roughly 26.5 metres by 14, are still clearly visible beyond the present pier among the stones. It is impossible to know whether the loose stones surrounding this structure have developed since the present harbour was built. If they predate the present harbour they would have made an unsuitable bottom for vessels alongside the pier. It is possible that the old pier might have been associated with a fish-trap structure; more probably, its primary function was to provide shelter for the bay and protection for a beach landing. Whatever the case, this pier is very old. Exactly how old is not clear, but comparison could be made with a recently-discovered medieval harbour at Cushat Stiel beneath Dunstanburgh Castle.

The L-shaped footings of a pier south-west of the present harbour, described as 'old' on Robertson's plan of 1759.

*Walk back past the limekilns and, immediately beyond them, turn right, so that the harbour is behind you.*

## Herring Houses

The row of red-tiled houses beyond the wall ahead of you to the left is 'Kippery Court', built between the Wars from the ruins of John Wood's herring yard. Throughout most of the 19th century Beadnell had two herring yards, sited here and at the present car-park. The two yards were operated in the mid 19th century by a branch of the Ewing family, who also developed the herring industry in Seahouses. By 1884 they had changed hands, and in 1910, shortly before their demise, the two yards were operated by Davidson, Grey and Co, and by Charles and Richard Dawson of Seahouses.

Herring landed from keelboats at the harbour were brought to the yards by horse and cart, and deposited through 'bowley holes' in the walls into troughs called 'farlins', where they were sorted into size. It was the women's job to sort and gut the herring, and to pack them into barrels with layers of salt, for export by ship from the harbour. Local women and girls were contracted to work for the season by the coopers who oversaw the herring yards. They worked in crews of three, two to gut and one to pack. At the busiest times, they were joined by Scottish fisher lasses, who were employed for the year, and who 'travelled the fishin's', following the herring shoals as they migrated down the coast from the North of Scotland in January to East Anglia in October. Some unmarried girls from Beadnell joined these fisher lasses, travelling south with them to Whitby and Great Yarmouth.

*Beadnell women at the herring c1905. From left: Maggie Jane Dixon, Bella Patterson, Bet Hall, Sal Fawcus and her daughter Bella, Hannah Hall. As a young woman Hannah 'travelled the fishin's' and, when World War I broke out, she is said to have asked: 'Is Yarmouth on wor side?'*

19

*It was once common to use upturned keelboats as sheds; examples can still be seen on Holy Island. This one, with Aa'd Steen (Tom Stephens) by the door, stood on the site of the present Beadnell Beach Guesthouse.*

There was more than one way to preserve herring. By far the greatest quantity was 'cured' as just described, with layers of salt in barrels for export to the Baltic. Smaller quantities were preserved by smoking. Traditionally, herring were roughly salted then smoked whole, sometimes for as long as several weeks. The process of 'kippering', or splitting the herring and smoking them for a much shorter period of around 16 hours, was introduced into the North East – some say invented – by John Woodger at Seahouses in 1843. This Beadnell herring yard included a large smokehouse. Beach Court guesthouse, the turreted building next to the row of cottages, is also built from stone from the yard. Before the harbour was built a 'yawl house' and cottage stood on the site, and white fish such as cod and haddock were dried on the sands. This was an ancient method of preserving them. When buildings at the new harbour were advertised for sale in 1800 they were described as adjoining 'one of the best fish-drying beaches in the country'.

***Take the track between the limekilns and the cottage wall, roughly east towards Ebb's Sneuk Point.***

Notice on your right the ramp up to the top of the kilns. This was wider in the past, allowing the horse-drawn railway from what is now Harbour Road to run to the top. Local folklore records that an unfortunate horse, unloading stone into one of the kilns, was backed up too far, and lost into it.

## Salt Cellars

To your left, at the back of Kippery Court at the edge of the sailing club, notice the small pan-tiled stone sheds. These were the salt cellars for the herring yard. The red pan-tiles are characteristic of ports in the area in the 19th century, when they were brought back from the Low Countries as ballast on sailing ships.

### Beadnell Sailing Club

Beadnell Sailing Club on your left was founded in 1935 following a highly successful Regatta that summer. Its founder and first Captain was Major H.L. Burton, G.C., O.B.E, who lived in a cottage on Harbour Road until his death in 1944. Major Burton was awarded the Empire Gallantry Medal, later changed to the George Cross, for his service on board the first motorised Tyne lifeboat, the *Henry Vernon*, at the rescue of the hospital ship *Rohilla* off Whitby in 1914.

*Major Burton taught a generation of holiday-makers' children to sail aboard his yacht, Wanderer, before World War II.*

**Walk past the cottages to your left and out along Ebb's Sneuk, taking care to remain on the footpath.**

# 3. EBB'S SNEUK

*Ebb's Sneuk, or Beadnell Point, belongs to Northumberland County Council, and the area includes a scheduled ancient monument. Although the Point is open to the public, great care should be taken not to stray off the path, as the sheer cliff is subject to erosion.*

## Sneuk or Neuk

The Sneuk is made up of sedimentary strata topped by massive limestone. Most of the foreshore which you see to the north consists of layers of Carboniferous limestone and sandstones, shales and fossil soils. There is a whinstone (dolerite) intrusion at Bent Hall, which, like the Farne Islands to the north and Dunstanburgh Castle Point to the south, forms part of the Whin Sill which runs across the country.

'Sneuk' is an Old Northumbrian word, meaning a promontory. Later Norse settlers adapted the name with their own variation, 'Ebba's Neuk'.

*The buried remains of St Ebba's chapel at Ebb's Sneuk.*

## St Ebba

Ebb's Sneuk takes its name from the Anglo Saxon Princess St Aebbe or Ebba, a contemporary of St Cuthbert in the 7th century AD. Ebba was the daughter of the first King of Northumbria. One of her brothers was the Christian King Oswald, who invited monks from Iona to send a mission to Northumbria. They established their centre on Holy Island, near the royal capital, Bamburgh, and from there encouraged the establishment of other monasteries. Ebba established Coldingham, an important monastic foundation to the north, near what is now St Abb's Head in Scotland.

## The Chapel

At the highest point of Ebb's Sneuk lie the ruins of a small medieval chapel and associated buildings, which date from about the 13th century. This is more than 500 years after Ebba's lifetime. Given Beadnell's proximity to Bamburgh and its administrative connections to the Anglo Saxon capital, it is possible, however, that a much earlier structure associated with St Ebba stood on the same site.

The rectangular chapel seems to have been surrounded by outbuildings and an enclosure. It could have been similar to the chapel and small monastic settlement on Inner Farne, which is visible from this site, and which probably dates from the same period. Written records from the 14th to 16th centuries show that the Farne settlement housed just one or two monks, and that these monks employed fishermen who used cobles, herring nets and long lines, much like the fishermen of Beadnell. Beadnell fishermen are also mentioned in the same records, carrying provisions and supplies of stone to the monks on Farne. Although there is no written evidence for monks at Beadnell at that time, it is quite possible that a similar tiny community of perhaps just one or two monks and their lay workers lived on this site. The 'old wall' shown on Robertson's plan of 1759, dividing the Ebb's Sneuk and harbour peninsula from the adjoining land, supports the argument that there might once have been a separate religious community here. Indeed, as we have seen, the name 'Beadnell' itself could relate to the word 'beadsman', meaning a man of prayer.

Until the mid 19th century Beadnell's parish church was at Bamburgh. St Ebba's Church in the centre of Beadnell was built in the mid 18th century as a 'chapel of ease', so that parishioners did not need to travel so far for services. Burials were recorded at Ebb's Sneuk until the late 17th century, but seem to have continued to take place after that. Ebb's Sneuk chapel eventually fell into disuse, and was covered in sand. It was excavated in 1853. Much more of the structure of the chapel was visible until World War II, when it was badly damaged by vehicles moving a heavy gun into position. The base of the concrete gun emplacement is visible just to the east of the chapel.

*Time Team's excavation of St Ebba's chapel in June 2011.*

In June 2011 Channel 4's 'Time Team' conducted a dig in and around the chapel ruins. They were hoping to discover the remains of an earlier, Anglo Saxon chapel beneath the medieval walls. The programme, which was broadcast in February 2012, showed that they found burials at several different levels: very close to the surface of the footpath, in the sand around the chapel, and under the structure itself. The dates of these burials will be announced in a forthcoming report. A trench within the chapel revealed a deep floor, which could predate the medieval period, and a later extension to the medieval structure at the east end. Most strikingly, the dig uncovered a number of infant burials just outside the chapel walls. These tiny skeletons suggest that, even after the 18th century church was built, Beadnell people continued to bury their children – perhaps unbaptised – in what they regarded as a special place. Many still feel it to be so.

A service is held on this site every year, either on St Ebba's Day, August 25th, or on the Sunday closest to it.

## Beadnell's First Limekiln

A little to the north-east of the chapel lie the remains of a circular stone structure, exposed by storms in the 1980s. An excavation in 1994 showed it to be a medieval limekiln, last fired between 1480 and 1510. Since then the structure has continued to erode and little of it is now visible.

*The partly-excavated medieval limekiln at Ebb's Sneuk, 1994.*

## Shipwrecks

Recognising the danger of Ebb's Sneuk to shipping, in 1828 Trinity House gave permission to John Wood to set up a beacon on the Sneuk during the herring season. We do not know exactly where this beacon was sited or what form it took. Even in relatively recent times there have been a number of recorded wrecks on the Point, most recently that of the British motor vessel *Yewglen*, which grounded on 29th February 1960 with a cargo of 1,000 tons of bagged cement, lime and French chalk. The crew were able to walk ashore to safety. Some of the *Yewglen's* remains may be glimpsed among the kelp to the north of the Point.

*M.V. Yewglen on Ebb's Sneuk, March 1st 1960.*

*Retrace your steps back along the Point until you come to an opening on your right. Turn right, then right again onto Harbour Road.*

## Seaside Vernacular

Before World War I there were no houses between the harbour and Bent Hall. Many of the houses along this stretch of Harbour Road were built between the Wars as holiday homes for prosperous Newcastle families, and represent various kinds of seaside architecture. The white house nearest the harbour, now called 'Beadnell Beach Guesthouse' or 'Low Dover', was a flat-roofed tea-shop run by Miss Dorothy Scarf. It was known locally as 'Dorothy's Café'.

*Proprietrix :* Miss R. D. SCARF

# DOROTHY'S
## ARTS AND CRAFTS

*The Mecca of Visitors for Morning Coffee and Afternoon Tea*

A LARGE SELECTION OF FANCY GOODS, NOVELTIES, VIEWS AND WATER-COLOURS OF THE DISTRICTS

On the dunes at the edge of the sea.

Hand-Painted China a Speciality
Leather Goods, Toys

**BEADNELL HARBOUR**
**Chathill : Northumberland**

*Phone:* Seahouses 291.     *Grams:* "Dorothys", Beadnell.

*An advertisement for Dorothy's Café from a 1950s guidebook.*

*A herring keelboat with its two distinctive sails depicted in stone – one of many local images in the garden walls facing Harbour Road.*

As you continue north along Harbour Road, look out for the simple shapes of sailing boats, fish and a butterfly in the stonework of the older garden walls. This was a local decorative tradition from the 1930s to 1950s. This area of Harbour Road changed considerably during that period. There is now little evidence to be seen of the old horse-drawn tramway which carried stone to the limekilns at the harbour, and nothing now remains of the 'old wall' shown on Robertson's map of 1759 as separating Ebb's Sneuk and the present harbour headland from the rest of the coast.

*Continue a little way along Harbour Road until you see a 1930s-style flat-roofed apartment building in front of you to your right. Stop before you reach this building, where the road curves to the left. You will see a row of older cottages built in the local sandstone in front of you to your left.*

## The White Rock Bronze Age Burials

On the right hand side of the road is a piece of land belonging to Beadnell Harbour Fishermen's Society. This was formerly the site of several fishermen's sheds. In 1934 workmen digging the foundations for these sheds discovered two ancient stone burial chambers, or 'cists', containing crouched skeletons. The burials are thought to date from the Bronze Age, around 3,000 years ago. The land is private and little remains to be seen of this scheduled ancient monument; but what is believed to be the cap-stone of one of the cists may be viewed from the road, at the foot of a stay-wire supporting an electricity pole.

Other ancient burials have been found elsewhere in Beadnell. More than half a mile to the north, on the camping site south of Link Cottage, opposite the inlet known as Collith Hole, workmen uncovered two burial cairns in 1970. The cairns were built over cists, apparently of Bronze Age origin. They had been used for multiple burials in the Iron Age, roughly 2,000 years ago. A cup-and-ring marked boulder of still more ancient origin was also found on the same site.

*Remain on Harbour Road, passing the row of cottages to your left, and stop near the road junction on the seaward side, with the little green to your left.*

*Boys with their model boats at Bent Hall, c 1900. Most of the cottages were occupied at this time by fishing families, including two households of Dixons and two of Liddells.*

# 4. THE BENTY

## Bent Hall

The rocky point on which the 1930s apartment block stands is called the White Rock. Behind you to your left are the cottages of Bent Hall, known locally as 'The Benty'. This name comes from the wild bent grass that grows by the sea. The cottages were built by the Wood family in the mid 18th century, on the site of an earlier Bent Hall. They are marked on the 1759 plan as 'Grey's Inn Houses'. Charles Grey, a relative of the Woods, was tenant there a few years earlier. The land and cottages eventually passed to Thomas Wood Craster.

Between 1841 and 1871, one of the cottages in this row was home to Alexander Ewing. Other members of this influential family had moved from Horncliffe to Seahouses, where they developed the herring industry. Ewing, who also farmed for a time at Bent Hall, leased the two Beadnell herring yards from Thomas Wood Craster. By 1870 Ewing was in debt, and his business was taken over shortly afterwards by other members of his family, and then by Henry Cowe, a fish curer from Leith.

*Beadnell women at the herring c1906. The woman with her hand on her hip, right, is Kate Stephens with, to her right, her sister Rachel, and mother, Mary Ann. Farthest right is Meg Beadlien. They stand outside the herring yard known as 'Glass's Shed' on the site of the present car-park.*

*Women gutting herring outside 'Glass's Shed' on the present car-park site.*

## Bent Hall Farm

Bent Hall was one of four farms in Beadnell in the 19th century. The others were Annstead (to the north of Beadnell village), Beadnell Town Farm and Beadnell Green. In 1842, Bent Hall consisted of 119 acres, belonged to Thomas Wood Craster and was farmed by George Manderson. By 1881, it was farmed by

Robert Wintrip, in 1902 the farmer was James Grey, in 1910, Ralph Scott and in 1921, James Kennedy. The middle cottage of the Benty row was the farmhouse. Bent Hall Farm was bought by the Davidson family in 1936. Until the early 1990s a milk pasteurisation and bottling plant stood next to the farmyard across the road. Black and white dairy cows grazed in the fields behind.

*Tom 'Skee' Hall's coble, Golden Horn BK75, at the Benty, c1920. Behind it stand James Kennedy's hay and corn stacks in Bent Hall farmyard.*

## The Benty Hole

On the seaward side of the road, where a band of darker rock cuts across the limestone, lies a narrow inlet known as the 'Benty Hole'. This darker rock is an intrusion of igneous dolerite, or 'whinstone', which pushed up between the layers of limestones and sandstones as magma (molten rock) during the Carboniferous period. It was later exposed by erosion. Like the Farne Islands to the north and Dunstanburgh Point to the south, it is one of the places where the Whin Sill which crosses the country reaches the sea.

The gap in this whinstone dyke is not a natural feature. In 1747, John Wood leased quarries on the Beadnell foreshore to George Turnbull of Cambois. Turnbull blasted through the whinstone to create a harbour, which he used to export stone. He also built a limekiln on the White Rock Point nearby. A large rectangular inlet in the White Rock probably also dates from this time. Turnbull's harbour predated the present one by about 50 years and was, for most of the 18th century, the main harbour of export for the quarrying and lime-burning operations in Beadnell. Robertson's map of 1759 shows a quay opposite the harbour entrance. The remains of this can still be seen among the loose stones. As well as the limekiln at the end of the point, the map shows the mysteriously-named 'Meg Lowrey's Lodge'.

*The remains of George Turnbull's mid-18th century quay at the Benty, once the main harbour for Beadnell, used for the export of stone.*

With the building of the new harbour in 1798, and the decline of the quarrying and lime-burning industries in Beadnell, the Benty harbour was no longer needed for its original purpose. But, as may be seen from the rusting winches across the road, it was used as a fishing harbour until recent times.

The Benty Hole is also known as the 'Nacker Hole', a name which is probably of ancient origin. It is possible that it might derive from the Anglo-Saxon word, 'nicor', which occurs in Beowulf and means a 'water monster'. An unusual rock formation such as a whinstone dyke typically inspired such names and stories.

The 'road to Alnwick' shown on Robertson's plan was no more than a track through the bent grass. Its remains can be seen in the footpath which runs along the links from the caravan site to the Long Nanny burn.

*Geordie Fawcus and George 'Young Punch' Dixon in the coble Meggie BK425, 1936. The man-made opening in the whinstone dyke formed a harbour, which continued to be used by fishing cobles until the 1960s.*

***Cross the road that leads to the car-park and continue along Harbour Road until you reach some public seats, near sheds and a bungalow on the seaward side. Stop at the seats and face north. These buildings and the row of houses on the left side of the road relate to the rocky peninsula just ahead of you. The grass field on this peninsula is private land.***

# 5. DELL POINT AND WINDMILL STEADS AREA

Roughly north of you is the promontory of Dell Point or Red Brae, and on the other side of the road a row of houses known as Windmill Steads. In the local dialect 'to dell' means 'to delve' or dig, and Dell Point was named after the extensive quarrying operations which were carried out along the foreshore in the 18th century. All around Dell Point, evidence of this work is still visible. It was said that so much limestone was removed from this headland that quarrying was halted for fear that heavy seas would damage the nearby kilns, salt pans and the harbour at the Benty.

The Dell Point quarries were leased by Thomas Wood to George Turnbull of Cambois in 1747, together with permission to erect limekilns. Robertson's map of 1759 shows a row of four kilns on the south side of the Point, with coal shafts and a windmill above them. The windmill was described in a lease as an 'engine belonging to the colliery', and seems to have served as a pump. The field immediately above Dell Point shows no surface evidence of the windmill, but remains of what is probably one of the limekilns shown on Robertson's map are visible in the south face of the cliff.

*The remains of an 18th century limekiln in the south face of Dell Point.*

## Windmill Steads

The name 'Windmill Steads', retained by the houses opposite, was originally given to a row of quarrymen's cottages, built by Thomas Wood in about 1766 on the site now occupied by the bungalow on the seaward side of the road.

These cottages were divided into an upper storey of three two-roomed dwellings accessed from the road, and a lower storey of three more which opened onto the beach. It was said that the sea frequently flooded the lower storeys. One of the last residents to have been born in the 'old Steads' claimed, no doubt with some exaggeration, that his mother rocked his cradle in the kitchen as it floated on the tide! The old Steads were abandoned in 1902 and their occupants, by this time mostly fishing families, re-housed by their landlords, the Crasters, in the present Steads opposite.

*Old Windmill Steads (above), first mentioned in the Parish Registers in 1766, and the 'new' Steads (below), which replaced them on higher ground in 1902. At that time Harbour Road was only a track, and the doors to the new houses opened to the west to protect them from the sea. The shed behind the new Steads was made out of box beds from the old cottages.*

Of the old Steads, only the stone stable now remains. In the early 20th century this was used by Jack Dixon, the local carter, who carried fish to Chathill station. Jack travelled slowly. His horse and cart occupied the whole road, and if a motor car drew up behind him, he refused to let it pass. 'Ye in a hurry?' he would shout. 'Ye should a got up earlier!' Today his old stable is used to store fishing gear.

*(Right) Carter Jack Dixon in 1927. He kept his rather tired-looking horse in the stable (below), which is all that remains of old Windmill Steads today.*

## Huts and Shiels

Next to the stone stable stands a working joiner's shop and, next to that, a 19th century tarred fisherman's hut of a kind which was once very common in Beadnell. These huts were used by fishermen to make and mend gear in winter. In the summer, fisher families often rented their cottages to holiday-makers, moving into these huts for weeks at a time. This practice provided much-needed extra income. Perhaps it perpetuated an ancient tradition of 'shieling', whereby fishermen took up summer residence in seashore huts called 'shiels'. The memory of this practice is preserved on Tyneside in the name North and South 'Shields'.

*Three Beadnell fishermen: Tom Fawcus with his father John ('Aa'd Weir'), and Bill Dixon, aged about four, in 1911, outside 'Aa'd Weir's hut'. This is one of the last of Beadnell's black huts, and is still in use by fishermen.*

## Salt Pans

In the mid 18th century salt-making was an important industry, particularly for fish processing; and salt was an expensive commodity. The shore to the south of Dell Point contained five salt pans, erected by Alexander Long of Sheerness, Kent, who also leased coal mines and a windmill from John Wood. According to the industrial archaeologist Stafford Linsley, Long seems to have introduced new salt-making methods into the North East, which involved concentrating the sea water by evaporation before boiling commenced. It is worth noting that, at St Monans in Fife, a windmill was used to pump sea water in the salt-making process; there is, however, no evidence to connect the windmill on Dell Point with the salt pans to the south. Another 18th century map shows a building marked 'Salt Office' on what is now Harbour Road. This could have been either the depot for the works, or possibly a base for the local Officer of the Salt, who was responsible for collecting the tax due on salt. Folk memory recalls that the northernmost part of old Windmill Steads was used for storing salt. No evidence of the salt pans is now visible on the beach.

*Continue further along Harbour Road, past Dell Point field to your right. Through the houses to your left you can glimpse the lake which occupies a former limestone quarry. Ahead of you are views to the Farne Islands, just clear of North Sunderland Point.*

*The remains of World War II defences in the north-east face of Dell Point.*

*Just north of Dell Point, a man-made line of stone blocks is often visible on the beach. These might be the footings of a jetty, or perhaps a low wall retaining a working platform to facilitate 18th century quarrying operations on the adjacent cliffs.*

**Continue past the first finger-post on the seaward side of Harbour Road (which marks the footpath running past the site of Beadnell Square). At the corner of Longstone Crescent, cross Harbour Road to the seaward side, where a second finger-post marks a footpath running down onto the beach. Pause here.**

# 6. BEADNELL HAVEN

Beadnell Haven was once the heart of the village's fishing industry. A sandy beach protected by rocky reefs, the Haven is a typical beach for landing and launching cobles. These natural conditions, and its location in relation to the rest of the village, suggest that it was in use from an early date. Considerable quantities of 'Bednelfysch' were sent to Durham Priory in the 14th to 16th centuries. It is reasonable to suggest that Beadnell Haven might have been one of the places where those fish were landed.

The Haven was certainly in use as a fishing place in the 18th century: Robertson's map of 1759 shows a 'fish house', possibly of medieval origin, on the site now occupied by the bark-pots to the south of the path. Until the late 1990s, cobles were still drawn up on the beach between the North and South rocks, and the land on either side of the footpath was occupied until recently by a number of tarred fishermen's huts, which were used both for storage and as workshops for making and mending gear. Two of these huts remain on the south side of the path.

*The Haven was, until the late 1990s, a busy site of fishing activity, which took place in and around the black huts. Here in winter-time the local fishing lore was passed on. (Photo: Tom Yellowley).*

*Beadnell Square, home to many fishing families, stood on the seaward side of Harbour Road, south of the remaining huts.*

## Beadnell Square

In 1777, John Wood built Fisher Square to the south of this site, as part of his great entrepreneurial enterprise. Typical of the architecture of local fishing villages at the time, the Square consisted of eleven two-roomed cottages, with a continuous overhead loft and a central courtyard. Similar examples, now much-renovated, may still be seen at Seahouses and, in a three-sided variation, at Low Newton.

It was typical of local landowners at this time to provide new, improved housing for their fishing families, away from the inland settlements and closer to their place of work. These 'sea houses' were found in many coastal villages, but it was only at the rapidly-expanding village of North Sunderland that the name stuck. 'Sea houses' like these were also intended to protect the gentry from the less picturesque aspects of fishing. In 1721 a Manor Court order prohibited Beadnell residents from the offensive practice of boiling fish-oil in their houses or in the town streets. By moving them closer to the sea, Wood removed the problem from under his nose.

In 1851 the eleven cottages of Fisher Square housed 48 residents. In the early 1920s at least one family of ten occupied two rooms. The adults and older children slept in 'box beds', large wooden cupboards with sliding doors, while the younger children slept on nets in the attic. The 'netties' (lavatories) stood on the bank-top, water was fetched from an outside tap, and there was no electricity. Families were re-housed in Longstone Crescent in 1938, and the Square was demolished shortly afterwards.

## Fishermen's Huts

Until the 1990s there were about eight huts on this site. Many of them were over 100 years old. The hut which still stands closest to the path was originally the 'Reading Room', provided in the mid 19<sup>th</sup> century by Wood's descendants, the Craster family, for the use of the village men. This was a common provision by landlords at the time, intended to keep the men away from the public houses. The Reading Room was stocked with newspapers and a billiard table. It also served as an isolation hospital during epidemics of diseases such as scarlet fever, a common childhood killer. It was given to the fishermen and became a privately-owned hut when the new village school and Reading Room opened in 1906.

*Fisherman Stephen Douglas in the doorway of the 'Reading Room' hut, 1992. 'Creeves' (crab pots) and 'tows' (ropes) are stacked outside.*

(Above) Stephen's brother, John ('Jack') Douglas, makes a 'creeve' inside the Reading Room hut, 1992. (Right) A third brother, Charlie Douglas, knits a creeve-cover inside his own hut, nearby. The men shared stories in the winter-time, among them that of the terrible blizzard of February 6th 1895, in which their father, uncle and grandfather almost lost their lives in their sailing coble, the Jane Douglas. They and many others were saved by taking shelter on the Longstone. The Seahouses coble Guiding Star was lost, along with two of her crew. Remembrance of such events down the generations helped to define the community.

***The land is privately owned, but there is a clearly-marked public footpath. Follow this footpath from Harbour Road to the beach.***

## Bark-Pots and Red Sails

To the right of the path lies a row of 'bark-pots', used until the 1960s to preserve natural fibre ropes and nets. At least three of the pots date from the late 18th century, and were probably contemporary with the Square. It is possible that they stand on the foundations of an earlier fish house, shown on Robertson's plan. Each consisted of a hearth with a chimney built of stone or brick and, above the hearth, a large metal tank, open at the top, like a big outdoor version of a wash-house set-pot. They were used to boil water and a tannin-rich substance, with which, before the introduction of man-made fibres, sisal and manila ropes

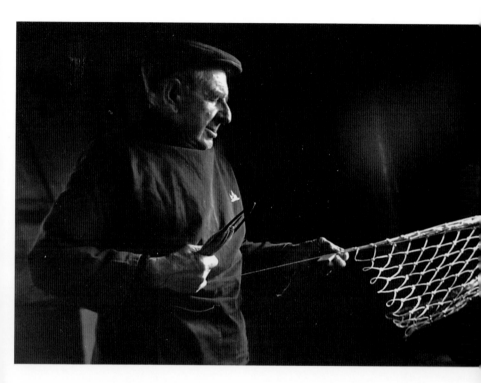

and nets were routinely treated. The tannin solution had astringent, degreasing and preservative properties, and was known as 'bark' because originally it was derived from oak-bark; but, from the later 19th century, fishermen used a substance called 'cutch', derived from the sap of a tropical plant [Acacia catechu]. Barking was an essential part of the fishermen's routine. Herring drift nets, for example, were barked every couple of weeks. Sails, and fishermen's smocks or 'slowps', were also sized and wind-proofed in this way – hence the traditional 'red sails' of the song.

After barking, ropes and twine were dried for some days, then tarred for further preservation. Most fishermen used old bark-pots for melting tar. At the height of their prosperity, each fishing village had several sets of bark-pots, each used by an extended family or a number of boats' crews. With the introduction of man-made fibres in the 1960s, however, bark-pots went out of use. The few remaining examples include, on Holy Island, a single brick-built pot next to the wall above the Ouse, and, at Craster, an in-filled bark-pot above the harbour. The row of Beadnell pots, with an additional, later, square-tanked pot next to it, is the best and possibly oldest example of bark-pots in north Northumberland. It is now a Grade II listed structure.

Beadnell had several sets of bark-pots, at the Benty, Haven and elsewhere. The photo to the left shows the bark-pots at the Haven. The photo below shows some Beadnell bark-pots in action c1890. A boy unloads coils of rope from a cart. Three men stand at the pot. One ladles the boiling 'cutch' solution over the ropes. Washing soda is added to the mix, and a man stands by with a bucket of cold water to prevent it boiling over. The Haven pots once had lids and high chimneys like this one.

## The Iron Man

On the other side of the footpath is a two-foot high iron capstan. This capstan, now missing its handle, was salvaged from a late 19<sup>th</sup> century herring drifter, where it was turned by hand to hoist the sail and haul the nets. An important piece of equipment in its day, it was known to fishermen as 'the iron man' and may be seen in action in the photo on p11.

*The 'iron man' capstan, half hidden in the long grass, bears the mark of its makers, Robertson Ltd of Berwick.*

***Walk down onto the beach and look out between the North and South Rocks of the Haven. It is recommended that you keep to the beach, as seaweed on the rocks is dangerously slippery.***

## Beadnell Haven

The traditional Northumbrian sea-boat, the coble, was developed to work from sheltered beach landings of this kind. It had a flat bottom aft, so it could easily be drawn up and launched from such sandy havens. In the past, cobles, and even the larger herring keelboats and smacks, were moored across the Haven overnight. The mooring rings and natural rock hold-fasts to which they were tied are now covered in seaweed and barnacles.

*Coble Jane Douglas BK115 moored across the Haven, 1990. Boat names were often handed down. This Jane Douglas, built at Amble in 1933, was the last of that name.*

*(Right) Cobles were designed to be launched from the beach. Even heavy, motorised versions, like the Golden Gate, were launched this way after their annual repainting, as in this photo (top) from March 1995. Each coble required the skills and labour of a whole community to maintain it. The small photos (below) show the same coble being hauled up three years earlier, using a hand winch and plenty of man-power.*

## Bratt Holes

A number of features of fishing archaeology are to be found on the North and South Rocks at low tide. Visitors are recommended not to venture out onto the rocks, however, as the seaweed is very slippery. Most striking among the remains are two rectangular troughs cut into the South Rock at the Haven's edge. The first trough measures approximately one by one and three-quarter metres, with a depth of about half a metre at the inner edge and quarter of a metre at the outer. The second is larger, measuring about one by two and half metres, with a depth of about half a metre. Each includes a sluice-hole, carefully cut to enable sea-water to wash in and out. These troughs were originally fitted with lids. They were cut in the late 18th century, as part of John Wood's great endeavour, The Northumberland Branch of the British Fisheries. The records of his enterprises state that 'hullies' were made to store live cod, lobsters and oysters. Two smacks were bought, the *Newcastle* and the *Experiment*, each of which was fitted with a well, and live cargoes were sent to Gravesend and Billingsgate fish market in London. In December 1790, the Society shipped 94,000 oysters and several hundred live lobsters from Beadnell to Newcastle. This large-scale trade was short-lived, but the troughs continued to be used in the 19th century to store live turbot or 'bratt', another high-priced fish which was carried live to London. The troughs were known among the fishermen as the 'Bratt Holes'.

'Hullies' continued to be used to store lobsters, before modern transport and refrigeration made it possible to carry them live to market by road. As late as the 1950s, lidded wooden 'hullie-boxes' were anchored in the 'Lobster Hole' towards the north edge of the North Rock.

*One of the 'Bratt Holes' or 'hullies' in the South Rock.*

## Long Lines and Mussel Holes

Until just after World War II, the staple form of fishing from all the Northumbrian villages between October and March was long lining for white fish such as haddock and cod. This was a labour-intensive form of fishing, carried out from cobles, usually crewed by three men, each working about a mile of line. Each line carried at least 1,400 hooks suspended from 'sneyds'; and each hook had to be baited every day with a mussel and a limpet. It was the women's job to bait the line for the next day whilst their men were at sea. They collected limpets from the rocks using a sharp blade called a 'picker'. Mussels were in shorter supply. Stocks were brought live to Beadnell by horse and cart from Waren, and later imported by train from Morcambe Bay, Cumbria, and Boston in Lincolnshire. Each family had their own mussel bed, and many of these beds lay between the South Rock and Dell Point, an area known as 'the Mushel Holes'. The mussels were laid here inside circular stone structures and kept in place by nets until they had developed natural hold-fasts. More than half a century after the last long line was baited at Beadnell Haven, little evidence of these circles can now be seen among the randomly scattered boulders.

*Kate (Stephens) Douglas and nephew Tom, baiting long lines at the Haven, c1914.*

*Another view of Beadnell Square in the early 1900s, showing the huts and bark-pot chimneys, and a coble in the Haven waiting for the tide. In the 18th century, kelp, a type of seaweed gathered from the shore, was burnt on the bank-tops. The sale of its soda ash as a fertiliser and for industry provided an important source of income.*

As you look out to sea, remember the generations of fishermen who sailed into and out of this haven. They carried in their heads an extraordinarily detailed knowledge of the sea floor, which was handed down from one generation to the next. They knew every rock, every clump of weed, every sandy, stony or muddy place on the sea bed; remembered who had caught what, where, and in what circumstances; and they could navigate back to those places by means of 'marks' – known points on the land, such as distinctive buildings, trees and hills, which they lined up to give an accurate position. This knowledge, with its detailed human stories and historical depth, cannot be replicated by the echo-sounders, position-finders and computer equipment which most boats now carry. Centuries old, it has been lost within the past 25 years, with the last generation of men who fished using long lines.

***Retrace your steps back along the path to Harbour Road.***

## A Mussel Shell Road

If you look closely you will see that part of the path is made up not only of sand, but of countless fragments of crushed mussel and limpet shells. These are testimony to the generations of women who worked long hours 'skeynin' (shelling) the mussels and baiting the lines. Each man's line took around three hours to bait, and a woman with several sons and no daughters often had to pay another to help her in this arduous work. Lines were usually baited in the back kitchen, although some of the fishing huts here at the Haven were used for this task. At one time, upturned herring boats were also used here as huts, as they still are on Holy Island.

'Dode' Hall, 1927. Like many fishermen, Dode smoked his clay pipe upside down to prevent sea-spray putting it out. He lived in the Square, where, in a time of austerity, he is said to have told his wife and her friend to 'sit and talk in the dark' rather than use up candles. The story reflects the hardships of the times. Dode was remembered with affection in the community.

*Cross the road and pause at the seats on the grassy area beside the telephone box. Facing towards the sea, with the shop immediately in front of you, Longstone Crescent behind you to your right and a road called The Haven behind you to your left, look left to the fenced green triangle between the roads.*

# 7. THE 'BULLRING' AREA

## 'The Bullring'

The triangular grassy picnic area and public space at the entrance to Harbour Road is known locally as 'The Bullring'. This is a relatively recent name. The area was refurbished by the Beadnell Jubilee Fund group between 2002 and 2005, and incorporates an anchor found by divers at the Farnes. Trees were planted in 2012 to mark the Queen's Diamond Jubilee. At one time this was a popular place for gypsies to camp on their way to and from St Boswell's Fair in the Borders. Until the end of the 18th century the road that runs north from Beadnell to Seahouses was merely a track through the dunes. John Wood improved communication between the two villages by building a bridge across the Annstead Burn in 1790. Nevertheless, as in many coastal villages, a friendly rivalry continued to exist with anyone who hailed from 'ower the born'.

*On the seaward side of Harbour Road, opposite the 'Bullring', George Patterson's bus depot, petrol station and garage operated from the late 1920s until the 1990s, when this photograph was taken.*

## Sea Breeze

The present shop opened in 1918 as Laidlers' 'Sea Breeze' shop and café. The building was originally a tarred hut which had served as an infirmary on Alnmouth links during World War I. Next to it is a fish and chip shop which operates in the summer months.

Harbour Road, August 1933, with Laidlers' shop to the left. The hut to the far right was George 'Steekie' Hall's smokehouse, improvised from an upturned herring boat.

The white Art Deco house on the corner of the road called The Haven was originally built as a butcher's shop and residence in 1936, and was named 'Rylands'. It became in turn Robinson's grocer's, Jimmy Lea's grocer's and post office, then served as a branch of the North Eastern Co-operative stores from 1953 to 1969. It has recently been extensively remodelled with an additional storey and is now a private house let out to holiday-makers. This photograph from 1936 shows Longstone Crescent being built behind it.

## Site of the Rocket House

Opposite the shop, at the south end of the Bullring, stood Beadnell's 'Rocket House'. This was built in 1867 to store the equipment of the local Volunteer Lifesaving Company. VLCs were formed all around the coast in the 19th century, in response to the large number of lives lost when ships stranded close to shore. Their work differed from that of the lifeboats, in that rescues were carried out from the shore, using a line carried by a rocket. Rescue was by means of breeches-buoy. This consisted of a lifebuoy equipped with a pair of canvas trunks, into which the wreck victims stepped. It was hauled back and forth along a hawser secured between the stricken ship and dry land. Beadnell did not have its own lifeboat; but in common with most coastal villages it did have a Coastguard. As part of his duties, the Coastguard was responsible for the VLC's apparatus and for training the crew. Lifesaving drill was practised at an exercise ground, with a 'Rocket Post' to serve as a ship's mast, at the Benty.

The last major rescue attended by Beadnell Lifesaving Company was that of the Norwegian motor ship the *Rask*, stranded on Scremerston Beach, Berwick on Tweed, on 31st January 1950. Berwick and Goswick Lifesaving Companies also attended. By this time Beadnell's Rocket House had already been demolished; but similar examples can still be seen at Craster on top of the Heugh, on Holy Island, and at Low Newton, where the local Rocket House has been converted into holiday accommodation.

*Fitting an iron 'plate' to a coble at the Haven, c1910. In the background is the 'Rocket House'. The joiner is probably Matt Summers, son of James.*

Beadnell Volunteer Lifesaving Company's rocket apparatus was transported by Dick Kennedy's horse and cart. One of the rocket practice-posts stood at the Benty.

Beadnell had its own football team. At one time the adult football field lay beside the vicarage and the school football ground was in Walter Anderson's field, now 'Hallgarth' house. This photo from 1948 shows: Back row, l-r: Joe Robson, John Breeze, John Dixon; Middle: Bill Liddell, Trevor Leightley, Billy Straughan, Selwyn Leightley, Margaret Hall; Front: Selby Allan, Hugh Stevenson, Joe Pearson, John Murray, Dougie Douglas.

# 8. BEADNELL HALL AND THE 'TOON'

*Turn left into the road called The Haven and, with the bus shelter to your right, walk up this road until you have crossed Meadow Lane.*

## The 'Toon'

You are now entering the old village, or 'toon'. The word 'toon' comes from the Anglo Saxon word for a settlement. In the early 18th century, Beadnell consisted of two rows of houses with a village green in the middle, complete with chapel, stocks for punishing offenders, and a pinfold for stray animals. There were five principle houses at that time, four of them clustered around the green. Although these houses were altered, and a larger church added in the 18th century, by 1860 the actual layout of the village does not seem to have greatly changed.

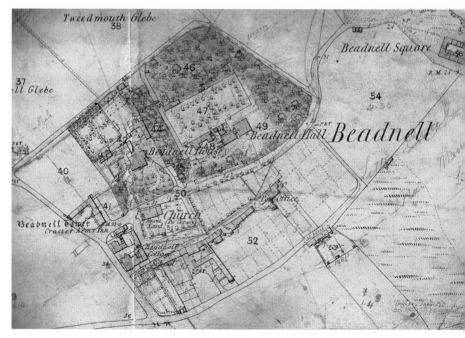

The first edition twenty-five inch scale Ordnance Survey plan, c1860, shows a large number of gardens in the centre of Beadnell. A document from 1856 among the Craster papers lists the allotment of 40 cottage gardens in the central village, with an additional two at Windmill Steads and five at Bent Hall. Farm labourers received much of their income 'in kind', and grew produce for sale on small-holdings such as these. Beadnell's fishermen also held gardens as part of their tenancy: the names of all 15 fishermen heading families in the 1851 census appear on the allotment list.

*Beadnell Hall in its heyday as an hotel just after World War II. During the War, the Hall and other Beadnell hotels and holiday houses were used as a billet for troops.*

## Beadnell Hall

Beadnell Hall stands on your right as you walk up The Haven towards the church. It is now surrounded by modern cottages. Originally known as the East Hall, this was the home of the landowning Forster, then Wood, families – including John Wood and his father Thomas. The Woods bought the Hall and large landholdings in Beadnell from the Forsters in 1735. Most of what you see here is 17th and 18th century; but the Hall is built on the site of a much older pele tower, which belonged to the Hardings, a Newcastle family who settled in Beadnell in 1383. Pele towers were fortified houses, built to withstand raids by the Scots. Part of the wall of this ancient tower remains, incorporated into the east side of the building.

When John Wood died in 1828 Beadnell Hall passed to his son, Thomas, who took his mother's name of Craster after he inherited the Craster estate in 1837. Thomas' wife was also a Craster. Another branch of the Craster family already owned the Annstead estate between Beadnell and Seahouses, which they had bought from John Wood in 1799. As Thomas Wood Craster also bought up Beadnell Town Farm from another branch of the Forster family, the Crasters now owned most of the land in Beadnell. Thomas Wood Craster lived in Craster village, and Beadnell Hall was let; in the mid 19th century the tenant was the vicar, and later a widow from the Forster family. By 1901 the Hall was home to Colonel William Craster. Before World War I, Colonel Craster invited all the Beadnell fishermen to Christmas dinner in the Hall every year, and the village children would visit at New Year to receive a penny each from him as 'Hogmanay'.

In the 1920s, the Hall was home to R.A. Dodds, head of a large butchery firm in Newcastle. Then, around 1930, it became one of several large Beadnell houses to be purchased and turned into an hotel by enterprising local fisherman Jack 'Aa'd Fid' Hall and his wife Annie. Beadnell Hall Hotel was later run by Jack's son, Hector, who, as 'late Solo Tenor of Christ Church Cathedral, Oxford, and a popular BBC artiste', offered concerts in the Music Room and nightly dances in the Ballroom. A brochure from the 1950s boasts of the hotel's 37 bedrooms and advertises a weekly tariff of between 14 and 18 guineas. Today the Hall is a Grade II listed building and is divided into private apartments.

## St Ebba's House and Cottages

Opposite the Hall is St Ebba's House. Once known as 'Ivy Cottage', this Grade II listed 18th century house belonged to John Wood and was leased as a holiday retreat in the early 19th century to Susannah, Lady Delaval of Ford. Lady Delaval was a colourful figure, a former mistress who became wife of the much older First Baron Delaval of Seaton Delaval Hall. After she was widowed she wore a black armband where, it was said, 'the Devil gripped her'. 'Ivy Cottage' appears as a post office on the 1860 Ordnance Survey; and by 1901 it was a lodging house run by Emma Davison. The two cottages adjoining it were the servants' quarters.

*St Ebba's House as a lodging house for holiday-makers in the early 20th century.*

***Continue up the road until you reach the churchyard.***

# 9. ST EBBA'S CHURCH, THE VILLAGE GREEN AND CHURCH ROW

## St Ebba's Church

St Ebba's Church was built by public subscription in 1746, on the site of an earlier chapel on the village green. Originally a simple structure, with no chancel, and a gallery at the west end, it was enlarged in the last decade of the 18th century. In 1854 Beadnell Parish was formed – Beadnell had hitherto been part of the Parish of Bamburgh – and a few years after that, in 1860, the church was largely rebuilt. It was given Gothic windows, gables and buttresses, and the spire was added, with its octagonal stone surround. Shortly after 1860, the vicarage – now, like the church, a Grade II listed structure – was built at the northern edge of the village on what is now the main road. Further alterations were made to the church in 1889, when the western gallery was removed, and in 1928-9, when a screen was added in memory of Mary Freeman of Beadnell House. The door was moved from the north to the west side around the same time.

*St Ebba's Church in the 1920s. The railings were removed for scrap metal during World War II. An early motor car stands outside the Craster Arms, and ale barrels lie at the roadside.*

*Renovating the church in 1889, looking west. The builders include Ned Fordy (far left), Bill and George Fordy (right), and three unnamed men in the rafters.*

The church contains memorials to several local families, including the Forster, Wood, Craster, Taylor, Howey and Allhusen families, and to the seven Beadnell men who died in World War I. In 1947 a new stained glass window depicting St Oswald and St Ebba was dedicated as a memorial to the nine men of the village who died in World War II. Among the notable memorials in the churchyard is one erected by public subscription to four members of the Fawcus family – Andrew (aged 50) and his three sons – who were drowned within sight of their home on 31st January 1885. Theirs was one of three Beadnell cobles lost between 1882 and 1889, with a total of ten lives. The small stone building at the south-westerly edge of the churchyard was the 'bier house', where the dead of the village would lie before burial.

*From the roadside, look to your left behind the churchyard. You will see a row of cottages, which include the former Town Farm and, at the top, the schoolhouse, separated from the church by a village green. If you wish, take a detour behind the churchyard onto the green.*

*Billy Patterson outside his cottage 'Iona' c1910, with the church in the background. The church door was originally situated on the west side, but was moved to the north for a time. It was moved back to the west side in 1928-9.*

## Beadnell Town Farm

The Town Farm, together with a large part of the land in the village, belonged in the 17th and 18th centuries to a branch of the Forster family, the Forsters of Warenford. The Forster coat of arms may be seen above the farmhouse door. The Town Farm land had been held in the 15th and 16th centuries by the Swinhoe family, but was bought up by the Forsters in 1593 and held by them until the 1820s, when Matthew Forster died without a direct heir. The farm was then bought by Thomas Wood Craster. The Tithe Award of 1842 confirms Craster's ownership. Beadnell farm, consisting of 104 acres, was at that time farmed by Frances Ostens. In 1881, the farmer was George Atkinson. He employed four labourers, male and female, on 120 acres. In 1910 the chief crops were barley, oats, turnips, potatoes and grass, and the farmer was James Murdy. Most of the cottages in Church Row were occupied in the 19th century by agricultural workers. The loft, accessed by steps at the top of the row, served as a granary.

In 1851, excluding the outlying settlement at Annstead, 27 people in Beadnell were listed as farm servants or agricultural labourers, in comparison with 18 listed as fishermen. Of the named agricultural labourers, five were female. In the 19th and well into the 20th century, farm labourers, or 'hinds', were taken on for the year at the annual Alnwick Hirings in March. Each male labourer was contracted to supply a female labourer, or 'bondager', and children were also expected to work in the fields at busy times. The 'flittin's', or moving of hinds' families between placements, occurred annually on 12th May, around the time of the old Whitsuntide holiday.

*The Forster coat of arms above the door to the former Town Farm, together with the family's Latin motto, 'Redde Diem' (meaning 'restore the day').*

The Town Farm stackyard, to the rear of Church Row, faced onto Meadow Lane and the 'new' school. After the farm ceased operation, it became a riding school, and is now a small housing development. These two photos show harvest time in the stackyard in the 1920s. In the top picture, a 'bondager', or female labourer, stands on top of the stack in her traditional costume of shady hat, blouse, long skirt and apron. The lower picture shows farm worker Tom Mitchell, with the hay 'bogey' (cart) laden with straw.

*A woman draws water from the pump on Beadnell village green c1910. Most cottages did not have running water until after World War I. Pumps like these were an improvement on the old village wells, like Crewe Well on Swinhoe Road, the Moor Well to the north, and the well on the links between the Benty and the harbour.*

## Crewe House – The Village School

Crewe House, the house to the south of the church on the south-west corner of the village green, was built by the Lord Crewe Trust as a school house in 1820. It served as the village school until 1906, and continued to house the village school-teacher until much later.

The Lord Crewe Trust was an important benefactor in the area. Nathaniel, Lord Crewe, Bishop of Durham, who married Dorothy Forster of Bamburgh Castle and bought up property in Northumberland and Durham from his wife's family, died in 1721 leaving no male heir. He left his property in trust for charitable purposes and a high proportion of the trust's income was used towards schools in the Bamburgh area. These included, from 1761, a free school within Bamburgh Castle itself, and from 1820 this school in Beadnell.

The school was conducted in a room at the top of the stairs. Seven poor children were educated free. The other children each paid 2d per week. The local vicar, and later the Craster family, also contributed financially to the running of the school. By the 1870s it had around 100 pupils. The school log books, held by Northumberland Archives at Woodhorn, make fascinating reading. They record in January 1886 that 'many parents keep no sort of register and only guess their children's ages.' When school fees were raised to 3d per week, many parents withdrew their children in protest. Attendance at the school dropped off considerably when children were needed for work, either in the fields or during

(Above and below) Crewe House, which served as the village school from 1820 until 1906. The house had a porch and steps outside, leading to the schoolroom. The porch is visible in the group photo (below), which was taken in the late 1890s and shows schoolmaster Frederick Leak and his wife with some of their hundred pupils.

the herring season. The log book for August 10th 1877 records: 'The attendance this week is very irregular, the reason is that when there are any quantity of herrings brought in by the boats, the children will not come to school.' In spite of the difficulties of getting children to attend regularly, in 1883 the school was enlarged to accommodate 110 pupils.

# 10. THE TOP OF THE 'TOON'

*From The Haven, with the church to your left, walk on to the road junction, passing a former shop and post office to your left, and Beadnell House and the Craster Arms to your right.*

## Jane Summers' Shop

The Summers family, who lived opposite the church, played a central role in Beadnell village life in the 19th and early 20th century. James Summers was the village joiner, coffin-maker and undertaker. His workshop, now a garage, stood directly opposite the bier house. James' twin brother, Gilbert, was a cooper, making herring barrels and overseeing one of the herring yards. James' wife, Agnes, was postmistress. Beadnell had its own sub post office from at least the 1860s, in various locations. For decades, Agnes Summers ran the post office from her family home, here, next to the church; and her unmarried daughter Jane Summers later continued this family tradition. Jane's brother John ('Jack') became the rural postman. Before World War I, another brother, Matt Summers, continued his father's work as joiner and undertaker.

*Joiner James Summers and his wife Agnes, postmistress, in 1886, with their children (l-r) Gilbert, Elizabeth, George (in doorway with his fiancée, Mary Jane), John (with stick), Anne, and Jane (with hat). Agnes is holding Matthew. A few years after this picture was taken another storey was added to their house (above right).*

The 'old' school (left), joiner's shop (centre) and post office (right), now with two storeys, c1910. The name on the side of the house is that of James Summers. His joiner's shop was used after World War II by Bill Liddell, who sold kippers and Sunday newspapers there.

Postman John ('Jack') Summers taking a shortcut along the beach, August 1927.

Most recently, Beadnell's post office was located in the Sea Breeze shop at the Haven. The post office's closure early in 2012 marked the end of 150 years of service. At the time of writing, the village is served two afternoons a week by a mobile post office.

## Beadnell House

This house was built by Richard Taylor in the mid 19th century on the site of an earlier residence. The Taylor family owned land in Beadnell from the 17th century, when they acquired it from the Forsters of Brunton, and they remained major landowners in the village until the early 20th century. Richard Taylor was married to Sarah Howey of the Pasture Hill estate near Seahouses, which included profitable coal mines, and Taylor developed the coal mines on his own land in Beadnell. The church and churchyard contain a number of memorials to members of the Howey-Taylor family. A sale notice of 1920 records that the house had ten bedrooms, three large reception rooms, two kitchens and servants' quarters – but only one bathroom. That was luxury by the standards of most cottages of the time, which had no running water. Beadnell House was occupied in the 1920s by the Freemans, a Newcastle family; then in the early 1930s it became the last of three big houses in the village to be converted into an hotel by the Hall family.

*Beadnell House, now divided into private apartments.*

## The Craster Arms

Like the Hall, the Craster Arms is built around a pele tower. It was built by the Forsters of Adderstone in the 16th century, and enlarged in the 18th century. It was known as 'Beadnell Tower', a name which, confusingly, still appears on some of the earlier Ordnance Survey maps. John Wood bought up its lands in 1783, but sold them off shortly afterwards to his brother-in-law, Edmund Craster of Preston, who became landlord of the Annstead estate. In 1818 the tower was operating as a public house called 'the Bull Inn', and by 1827, when the landlord was George Fordy, it had taken the name 'the Craster Arms'. By the mid 19th century, the Craster family owned much of the land in Beadnell and they remained major landlords in the village until after World War II. The Craster Arms remains a popular public house and is a Grade II listed building.

*The Craster Arms. When the North Eastern Railway opened up the coast to holiday-makers in the mid 19th century, one visitor to this inn wrote enthusiastically: 'No seagull eggs to cause me grief, Just good, substantial English beef.' John Ross was the proprietor in 1901.*

The coat of arms on the front of the pub is that of the family from which it takes its name, the Crasters. It shows the Craster 'Craa' (crow) and the motto 'Dum Vivo Spero' – 'While I live, I hope'.

The late 18th century cottages to the rear of the Craster Arms are known as 'the Curtain'. This name was often given to squares or rows of cottages enclosing unroofed yards. The Curtain was altered in the 19th century, and is now Grade II listed. After World War II, one of the cottages housed a private school run by Miss Gibson. This photo was taken c1914. The frame hanging from the cottage wall above the cart was used for making 'proggy' and 'clooty' mats from scraps of wool and rags.

**Stand at the road junction with the Craster Arms on your right.
The road ahead of you is called 'The Wynding'.**

## The Coastguard and Police Houses

The road to the right, leading out of the village, used to be known as 'Miss Amy's Hill' after Miss Amy Craster, who lived between the Wars in the house called The Wynding at the end of the road. When you stand at the junction, immediately ahead of you on the opposite side of the road you will see a pair of semi-detached cottages. These belonged to the Taylors of Beadnell House and were occupied from the late 19th century until the inter-War years by the village Policeman and Coastguard. Beadnell had a Coastguard Boatman, George Moyes, at the time of the 1861 census. A Police Officer first appears in the census for Beadnell in 1891. The Coastguard's duties included overseeing the Volunteer Lifesaving Company and deterring salmon poachers and smugglers. Smuggling had long been a problem on the Northumberland coast. The imposition of high import duties to pay for foreign wars in the 18th century led to widespread tax-avoidance. In September 1762, some 2,700 gallons of brandy, 400 of rum and gin, and wine, tea and other articles were confiscated from Scottish smugglers in Beadnell Bay. Local testimony records that disused coal workings along the links were used to hide smuggled goods in the 19th century.

*The Beadnell sword dance was performed by local fishermen on Old Year's Night and at Beadnell Feast. They practised in 'the Curtain'. The participants here include (l-r) Bob Fawcus, Dode Hall, Jack Hall, Hugh Patterson, Geordie Markwell (in drag, as 'Bessie' with umbrella) and one of Jack Hall's brothers, possibly 'Skee'. The picture is one of a series taken just before World War I.*

If you wish, you can take a detour here by turning right onto The Wynding, walking down the hill, and turning right again onto the main road, the B1340. From here, on the left side of the road, you can view the mid 19<sup>th</sup> century vicarage, now a private house; and among the trees a little further on, a mid 20<sup>th</sup> century AA telephone kiosk – now a rare survivor. Both of these are Grade II listed buildings.

*From the junction of The Haven and The Wynding, with the Craster Arms to your right, turn left onto The Wynding. On your left you pass Rose Cottage and Beadnell Towers Hotel.*

## Rose Cottage

In the early 1900s Rose Cottage was Edward Patterson's grocery store, and in the 1920s to '40s it was a general store and village post office run by his daughter, Dinah Patterson. It became a post office again in 1953. It is now divided into private houses.

*Dinah Patterson's store a few years after World War II. Bill Liddell's kipper boxes wait to be driven to Chathill station for the London train. The AA marker on the post office reads 'London 320 miles'.*

## Beadnell Towers Hotel

Originally a granary, this Grade II listed building became known as Beadnell Cottage in the 19th century. It was the residence of the Allhusens, an Anglo-German family who, having prospered in the grain trade, expanded into soap and chemical manufacturing on Tyneside. The house became an hotel under the ownership of the Hall family between the Wars. The proprietor was Jack's son, John Hall, then John's son, James. It is still a popular hotel today.

*Beadnell Towers as a two-storey private house, c1900. The Allhusens' cook, Maria Kirsop, stands at the door. A third storey was added when the house became an hotel.*

# 11. 'THE WHITE-WASHED CORNER' AND THE BIG FIELD

*The next T-junction was known locally as 'the White-Washed Corner', because the wall used to be painted white for visibility before the days of street lights. On your left is Meadow Lane, once known simply as 'the Lonnen', and on your right, Swinhoe Road, the old main road out of the village. On Meadow Lane just to your left is Alexandra House, with a newer cottage in front of it, and beyond it, the former Village School and Reading Room, with a children's playground behind it. You can if you wish take a detour a little way down Meadow Lane, returning to the T-junction to resume the walk.*

## Alexandra House

Alexandra House was built as an hotel by fisherman Jack Hall and his wife Annie in the first decade of the 20th century. It was the first of this couple's hotels, and they named it after the Queen Consort, Alexandra, wife of Edward VII. Jack was a much-loved character, extremely popular for his hospitality, and well-known for his affinity with animals. It was said that here, in the early years, 'banties' (bantum hens) roosted on the picture rails! Jack also owned a 'cuddy' (donkey) and a bad-tempered monkey called Jacko, which threw a tin of Brasso onto the stove and blew it up! Alexandra House was later managed by Jack and Annie's daughter, Mrs Annie Allan. It was badly damaged by fire in the early 1950s and subsequently renovated. It is now divided into private apartments.

*Alexandra House as an hotel between the Wars.*

*A view along Swinhoe Road towards the village. This was the main road into Beadnell until the B1340 by-passed the village, c1939. Most of these houses were built as holiday homes in the 1920s and '30s.*

## The 'New' School and Reading Room

The new Beadnell Church of England Public Elementary School opened in June 1906, as part of a wave of renewal occasioned by the 1902 Education Act. The land was given by the Taylor family, and the cost of the building – nearly £1,000 – was covered by the Craster family. The head teacher, Mr Frederick Leak, transferred from the old school, and the average attendance was 86 children. A new Reading Room attached to the school replaced the black hut at the Haven. Children at this school were taught in two classrooms until the leaving age of 14. Some who passed scholarship exams at the age of 11 went on to attend grammar school in Alnwick; for others, this was too far to travel. The 1944 Education Act raised the leaving age to 15 and made secondary education in separate schools compulsory. However, it took many years to fulfil the act in rural areas. Initially, older Beadnell children travelled to North Sunderland one day a week for cookery and woodwork. It was not until 1954 that they began to receive full-time 'secondary' education at North Sunderland. Beadnell Church of England Junior and Middle Infants School closed in July 1984, with just 17 pupils. Children from the village today travel to Seahouses and Alnwick for their education.

Immediately opposite the school, you can see another view of the Town Farm and its former stackyard, now a little cul-de-sac of houses.

*Beadnell school in 1935. To begin with, boys and girls were separated outside the classroom, with the boys' playground west of the school and the girls' in front of it. The teachers in this photo are (left) Miss Morgan and (right) Mr Hails.*

*The school building is now much-altered, and a private residence. The children's playground behind it was recently renovated after a massive local fundraising effort.*

## Beadnell Women's Institute Hall

The Women's Institute Hall is the long wooden building with the distinctive 'coble' weather-vane, almost opposite the former 'new' school. Northumberland Federation of Women's Institutes was first established during World War I, to revitalise rural communities and to encourage women to become involved in producing food for the War effort. Beadnell Women's Institute was formed in May 1923 in the Craster Arms. By the end of that year it had 36 members. Ever since, the W.I. has served an important role in Beadnell's community life, holding regular fêtes, talks, outings and charity fund-raising events. The W.I. Hall, built in 1925, now doubles as a village hall, and may be hired for events.

### BEADNELL GINGER BREAD.

½-lb. PLAIN FLOUR.   ½-lb. GROUND RICE   4-ozs. FAT.
1-gill of MILK.   or SEMOLINA.   2 teaspoonfuls GINGER.
1 teaspoonful CARB.   4-ozs. GOLDEN SYRUP   ½ teaspoonful MIXED
of SODA.   or TREACLE.   SPICE, if liked.
2-ozs. SUGAR.

Mix all dry ingredients together, leaving Bicarbonate of Soda to mix with warm Milk, melt Fat and Syrup in a pan, also Milk, leaving a little to mix with Soda. Add to dry ingredients and mix well, adding Soda last to make a nice thick batter, bake in a flat tin for ¾-hour in not too hot oven.—A. LIDDELL.

*A recipe from the Beadnell Women's Institute Silver Jubilee Cookery Book, May 1948. Produced under post-War rationing, the book contains recipes for treats such as 'Austerity Shortbread', and a recommendation that 'If mustard is eaten with kippers, it will stop them from reproving.'*

*At the T-junction from The Wynding, cross Meadow Lane and take the road ahead of you, slightly to your left, signed 'Kennedy Green'. Follow this road past Alexandra House and its adjacent cottages, past the children's playground and, skirting the edge of the new estate of Kennedy Green, follow the footpath into the field. Please close all gates, keep to the footpath while crossing the field, and take care not to disturb livestock.*

## Mr Howey-Taylor's Big Field

This field and the one to the west belonged in the 19th century to the Taylor family of Beadnell House. This one was known simply as 'the Big Field'. As you walk south across it, along the footpath to the caravan site, notice the rippled effect of 'rig and furrow'. The broad 'rigs' may be of medieval origin. They were probably ploughed as arable 'strips' in an 'open field' system, by peasants labouring for the local landowners in the centuries before enclosure.

# BEADNELL FEAST SPORTS

The Obstacle Race.

Fun In The Sack Race.

The Ladies' Tug-o'-War.

*Beadnell Feast, 1937. Originally held to mark the end of the herring fishing around September 20th, the Feast included a fun-fair with roundabouts, a shooting gallery and 'cuddies' (donkeys) on the village green. Sports for adults and children took place in the 'Big Field'.*

## Beadnell Green

Across the field to the right is Beadnell Green. This cottage was built in the mid 19th century. It was the farmhouse for the land around it, the Taylor family's 78 acre holding, which was the smallest of the four farms in the village. It was farmed in 1881 by Adam Smith and his family, with no hired labour. Its last farming inhabitants were Dick and May Kennedy, after whom Kennedy Green is named. The land to the west of the cottage was known as 'Dickie's Rashers' (rushes). May left in 1968, some years after her husband's death, donating to the school the piece of land which is now the children's playground. The farmhouse and buildings stood empty for many years, before recently undergoing extensive renovation as private houses.

In the early 1980s plans were submitted for a large housing development in the field through which you are now walking. The original plans incorporated a supermarket and leisure complex. A later version of these plans was passed, in spite of strong local opposition, but they eventually lapsed without any building taking place. The field now belongs to Northumberland Estates and is farmed as part of the Annstead holding.

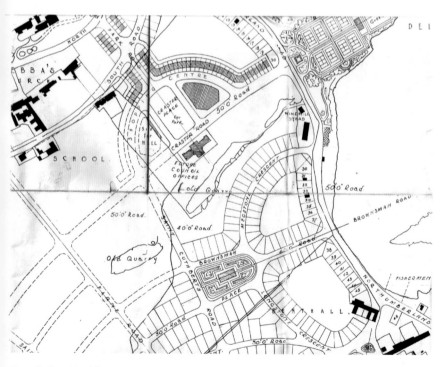

*Even before World War II, proposals were put forward to 'develop' Beadnell as a holiday resort. This plan extract from 1937, never realised, shows a large number of housing plots, a 'shopping centre' and 'future council offices'.*

A great deal of building has taken place in Beadnell in the last half century. It is difficult to imagine that the village and harbour were not joined with houses until after World War II. The estates of houses to your left, behind Harbour Road, are made up of several stages of development, each of which has altered the character of the village. The Longstone Close and Longstone Park developments were built in the late 1960s and early '70s. Although originally intended only for holiday use, they gradually evolved into residential properties. The Longbeach and Cardinal Point (St Ebba's Way) developments were built in stages over more than a decade. The final stage was completed in 2011.

## Quarry Pond, Kiln and Colliery

In the distance to your left you can glimpse the space occupied by the lake which lies between Longstone Park and the new Cardinal Point development. As we saw from Harbour Road, this was originally a limestone quarry. It appears to originate from the 1840s, and tallies with a revival in Beadnell's lime industry at that time. By the end of the 19th century it was long-disused and had filled with water. A report in the *Berwick Advertiser*, September 20th 1901, tells of a Scottish herring lass, Jane Cunningham, who was 'found drowned' in the pond. Her body was recovered by local fishermen using grappling irons.

*The remains of the limekiln adjoining the quarry and coal-shaft. Older Beadnell inhabitants recalled their fathers' stories of pitmen who lodged in the abandoned kiln next to the colliery in the 1890s.*

*Another limekiln stood on the links across the road from the present camping site. It was demolished before World War II. It seems to have been of the same design as the limekiln in the Big Field, and shows how that kiln might have looked.*

A limekiln adjoining the quarry may be seen from the footpath. It is probably of similar date to the quarry and therefore slightly later than those at the harbour. It is already described as an 'old kiln' on the 1860 Ordnance Survey. Just behind it lies the capped shaft of Beadnell colliery. Coal was needed for lime-burning, and there were coal workings in several places in the village. This one continued to operate commercially long after the village's limekilns had fallen into disuse. The colliery belonged to Mr Howey-Taylor of Beadnell House in the 1880s, and was sold to V.W. Corbett and Co in the 1890s. Two seams were worked, the Main Coal, which was abandoned in 1891 due to too much water, and the Beadnell Seam, which proved unprofitable. In 1896 it employed eight men underground and four on the surface. The colliery closed in June 1897.

## A Reminder of World War II

To the left, between the footpath and the limekiln, you can see a small concrete construction: a World War II 'pill box', built as part of a chain of defences along the coast. Following the defeat of the French and the evacuation of British troops from Dunkirk in June 1940, Britain faced Germany alone, and the terrifying prospect of invasion seemed imminent. As part of the response to this, thousands of such 'pill boxes' were hurriedly positioned around Britain's coastline, to provide 24-hour surveillance by the regular army and local defence volunteers, watching for any attempt at a landing by sea or air. Beadnell's beaches were closed to the public, surrounded by barbed wire, and minefields were laid. Searchlights were positioned at the Long Nanny burn, and possible exit-points from the beach were covered with pill boxes, anti-tank blocks and even, at the burn, old motor cars, intended to prevent landings by enemy aircraft. Periodically, the rusting remains of some of these vehicles still emerge from the sand.

The risk of invasion persisted until the winter of 1944. After the War, the pill boxes on the dunes gradually subsided and became unsafe, and they were removed or destroyed in the 1970s. The remains of two are still visible beneath Featherblaa' dune and at the Long Nanny. The pill box in this field, of prefabricated construction, belonged to a second line of defence, covering exit-points from the beach. Others in the series are visible at Swinhoe and Embleton.

*The World War II pill box, although a utilitarian structure, has an idiosyncratic touch: while the concrete was still wet, some local wit christened it 'Farne Hotel' after a popular Seahouses hostelry!*

## The Pond

Clay pits and a small brick-works lay along the edge of what is now Beadnell Bay caravan site from the mid 18th to the 19th century. They are marked on the First Edition Ordnance Survey, beside a cottage called 'Link House,' close to an 'Old Engine House', which might have belonged to further coal workings. Most of the clay pits have now been filled in. On the right side of the footpath across the Big Field, near the gate to the caravan site, lies a little pond, which might have been another quarry or, more probably, a clay pit. It has a tragic story connected to it. Beadnell school log book, January 30th 1891, records that three children from the neighbouring settlement of Tughall drowned here while walking home from Beadnell school. Matthew Thomas Turnbull, aged 9, and Thomas Simpson, a widowed shepherd's son, were sliding on the ice when they fell in. Matthew's older sister, Mary Ellen Turnbull, aged 12, went to the boys' aid, but also drowned in her attempt to save them. A memorial to the children erected by public subscription was one of the first monuments in Beadnell cemetery adjoining the vicarage, off the B1340 to the north of the village.

The memorial to the Tughall children who drowned in the pond in 1891. The inscription is now so worn that parts of it are illegible.

83

# 12. THE CARAVAN SITE

*Exit the field through the kissing-gate, and follow the path to the left through the caravans and back to the car-park.*

## Beadnell Links and Beadnell Bay Caravan Sites

In the early 20th century there were a number of small wooden beach chalets in the dunes at Beadnell. With the increasing availability of the motor-car between the Wars, camping and caravanning became more popular. Facilities were primitive. James Hall, hotelier at Beadnell Towers and grandson of Jack 'Fid' Hall, recalled that, even after World War II, caravan toilets were emptied onto a horse-drawn cart and the contents dumped in a nearby field. In 1958, James formed a company with the intention of setting up a first class static caravan park for the village. 'Beadnell Links' became the first of several such parks in Beadnell.

*The camping ground in the late 1940s. Beadnell Green Farm, then occupied by Dick and May Kennedy, is visible in the distance to the left.*

## Beadnell Today and Tomorrow

Over the last 250 years Beadnell has witnessed great changes. The noise, dust and smoke of its quarrying, coal mining and lime-burning industries in the 18th century, and the sheer numbers of incoming boats and people involved in its herring industry at times during the 19th century, meant it was not always the peaceful rural village which some imagine. In the 21st century, the issues facing the village are different, but equally pressing.

Today Beadnell's main income derives from its long-standing holiday and leisure industries. Beadnell depends on its visitors, and warmly welcomes them; but these industries bring their own environmental consequences. In particular, large-scale house-building has had a huge impact on the village in recent years. The current resident population, a large proportion of which is retired, is estimated to be around 550 – nearly twice that which depended on fishing and farming a century ago. Besides this, the village is currently said to have one of the highest ratios of holiday houses to year-round occupancy anywhere in the country, reported to be between 50% and 60%. Successful efforts have been made in recent years to encourage affordable housing, and thereby enable young working families to settle in the village.

*The quarry lake from the back of Longstone Park, 2006, with The Steads and Harbour Road in the background. The barley field has since been 'in-filled' with the Cardinal Point (St Ebba's Way) development.*

While Beadnell continues to change, residents and visitors agree that it is special. Why? What gives it its distinctive character and makes it different from everywhere else? Each person's answer to that question will be different; but most would agree that Beadnell's striking features include its small harbour and fishing boats, and the tranquillity and natural beauty of its beaches. It is the interaction between these elements, human and natural, that combine to give it a sense of 'place'.

Above all, whatever industries have come and gone in Beadnell, there is one that has formed its character more than any other. That is the community of small-boat fishing families. Over the centuries until recent times, in spite of attempts to industrialise it, this artisan fishing community changed very little. Its families shared a common purpose and – notwithstanding local disagreements and family feuds – a particularly strong sense of community. It is important not to romanticise the past. Theirs was a hard, dangerous existence, and no one would wish to return to the privations of the long lines or a winter weathered in an open coble. But fishing has left a strong imprint upon Beadnell, proving over centuries a sustainable way of life, long before that fashionable term was invented.

Artisan fishermen still work from Beadnell harbour. Their craft embodies skills, traditions and words which are as important to Northumberland's history as its castles and abbeys – perhaps more so. This is history, not as a museum exhibit, but as a living force, which, together with farming, continues to inform the experience of those who come to Beadnell as visitors or residents. Cynics have forecast the end of fishing in Beadnell for generations; the harbour is a constant drain on the resources of such a tiny community, and fishermen often struggle to make a living. Nevertheless, at the time of writing there are more boats fishing from Beadnell harbour than there were twenty years ago. As long as a small-boat fishery remains in the village, it reminds us of the inextricable connection between people and the natural environment, and the ways in which history connects all of us to place. It is a living example of the values – small-scale, and rooted in deep local knowledge and respect for the environment – by which Beadnell's unique character will continue to evolve into the future.

The harbour requires constant maintenance from the effects of storms like this one, in March 2008.

## The Blue Lonnen

The crunch of mussel shells under the boot heel;
The bramble-patch where the cottages were rooted;

The stone ring of the mussel bed, the stair
To the drying-green, the ballast heap, the beach of creeve-stones;

The tarry stain where the bark pot reeked; the wicket
In the wall; on the bridge to the limpets, the blade-worn groove;

The iron pin that marks the sea-road to the haven;
The nail driven into the door jamb – they are illegible

Without the rudder and the anchor,
Without the twine, the needle and the knitter:

For these are the paths they beat to the shore – The Nick. The Blue Lonnen –
And each is a road with a boat at the end of it.


Katrina Porteous, 2007

*Beadnell salmon fishermen at their nets in 2011. This is a low-impact and sustainable method of fishing. Materials might have changed, but the sight of small boat fishermen at their nets in Beadnell Bay is at least as old as Dunstanburgh Castle in the background.*

## Further Reading

Most of the information in this book is derived from Katrina Porteous' first-hand research conducted among key memory-holders of the village in the 1990s, and from her supplementary research conducted in local archives, including censuses, parish registers, directories, newspapers, maps, fishing boat registers and, most importantly, the Craster papers held by Northumberland Archives at Woodhorn.

Published primary sources include: J.T. Fowler, *Extracts from the Account Rolls of the Abbey of Durham* (Surtees Society, 99, 1898); and J. Raine, *The Charters of Endowment, Inventories and Account Rolls of the Priory of Finchale* (Surtees Society, 6, 1837). Important secondary sources include: E. Bateson, *Northumberland County History, vol. 1* (Newcastle, 1893); E. Craster, *Beadnell in the 18th Century* (*Archaeologia Aeliana*, 34, 1956, 161-173); and George Muirhead, *The Fishing Industry of Northumberland and Durham 1790-1914* (unpublished PhD thesis, University of Newcastle 1992).

Good recent books on the area include: Stafford Linsley, *Ports and Harbours of Northumberland* (Tempus 2005); Maureen Brook, *Herring Girls and Hiring Fairs* (Tyne Bridge 2005); Dinah Iredale, *Bondagers* (Glendale Local History Soc. 2008); and Caroline Hardie and Sara Rushton, *The Tides of Time: Archaeology on the Northumberland Coast* (Northumberland County Council 2000).

Katrina Porteous' own publications on Beadnell include: *Beadnell – a history in photographs* (Northumberland County Library 1990) and *Beadnell Harbour 200th Anniversary* (Harbour in Trouble 1998). In 2003 Katrina published *The Bonny Fisher Lad* (The People's History), a record of memories from the north Northumberland fishing community, which includes many first-hand accounts and photographs from Beadnell fishermen; and in 2007 she edited *Clarty Boots and Inky Fingers* for the Old Parish of Bamburgh Local History Archive, which includes oral history and photographs from Beadnell school.

Katrina's articles about Beadnell history have been widely published, notably in *Archaeology in Northumberland* vol. 17 and 18, 2007 and 2008; and in *North East History* vol. 37, 2006. Her research paper co-written with Dr Adrian Osler, '*Bednelfysch and Iseland Fish*': *Continuity in the Pre-Industrial Sea Fishery* of *North Northumberland 1300-1950*, was published in *The Mariner's Mirror* vol. 96, no. 1, Feb 2010. Her work on dialect in the Beadnell fishing community is included as Appendix 1 in Bill Griffiths' *Fishing and Folk* (Northumbria University Press 2008). Katrina's poems about the Beadnell fishing community can be found in *The Lost Music* (Bloodaxe 1996), *The Wund an' the Wetter* (Iron Press 1999) and *The Blue Lonnen* (Jardine 2007).

The text of *Limekilns and Lobsterpots* is based on one of a series of 'Local Heritage Walks' led by Katrina Porteous and former National Trust Archaeologist Harry Beamish for Northumberland Coast AONB Partnership between 2006 and 2010.

*173 years of Beadnell history: Katrina Porteous with Tom Douglas (left) aged 88, and his brother Charlie Douglas, aged 85, in spring 1995.*

Two views of Beadnell from Swinhoe Road, taken roughly 100 years apart. In the top picture, c1912, Alexandra House and the 'new' school stand alone at the far right. The old 'Crewe Well' lay at the left side of the road, west of the 'hemmel' (cowshed). In the later picture (2012), the hemmel has been converted into a guesthouse of the same name, Beadnell Towers has grown another storey, and the village has expanded to the west and south. St Ebba's Church and the Craster Arms are still clearly visible.

## Acknowledgements

While every effort has been made to obtain permission for the use of photographs, and to provide correct information, please accept my apologies for any permissions which I have inadvertently overlooked or mistakes which might have occurred. I would be very grateful if you would notify me of these via my web address: info@katrinaporteous.co.uk. I should like to thank everyone who has contributed photographs and information to me over the past 25 years. Although these are too many to thank individually, special thanks go to Catherine Petty and her late mother, May Douglas; to the late fishermen Charlie Douglas and his brothers, Tom, Stephen and Jack, and cousins Bob and 'Benty' Jack; to John and Kathleen Dixon and the late Maisie Bell; to Jennifer Hall and her late parents, James and Molly; to the late fishermen Bill Smailes of Craster and Redford Armstrong of Amble; to David Horsley for the use of photographs taken by his late father, Tom; to Tony Law, Peter France and Dr Tom Yellowley; to Hector Handyside, master coble-builder; to my own Father and Mother, Dr Ian and Joan Porteous; to Linda Bankier at Berwick Archives; to all the members of Old Parish of Bamburgh Local History Archive; and to the staff at Northumberland Archives at Woodhorn. Particular thanks to the Craster family for permission to use James Robertson's plan (NRO ZCR 5). Lastly, thanks to Paul Rea at Red Square Design and Vicki Whetstone at Potts Print (UK) for their work in the final stages of this book, and to my friends: Catherine Dodds for designing it; James Dodds for his assistance in co-publishing it; Mary and Stuart Manley at Barter Books for their artistic advice and commercial support; and former National Trust Archaeologist Harry Beamish for his unfailing knowledge, good humour and kindness throughout.

May Douglas (1920-2009) was one of the last fishermen's wives to knit a 'gansey' (fisherman's jersey), and the last in Beadnell to bait a long line. She was also Beadnell's unofficial archivist and an inspirational speaker on local history. Her love of the village led her to serve on the Parish Council, Parochial Church Council, as a school governor, and for 21 years as President of Beadnell Women's Institute. In 1990 she was honoured as a recipient of Maundy Money from the Queen. This book is dedicated to her memory.